MIRIAM RIEBACK

The Balancing Act

Poems for the weary soul

This book was professionally typeset on Reedsy.
Find out more at reedsy.com

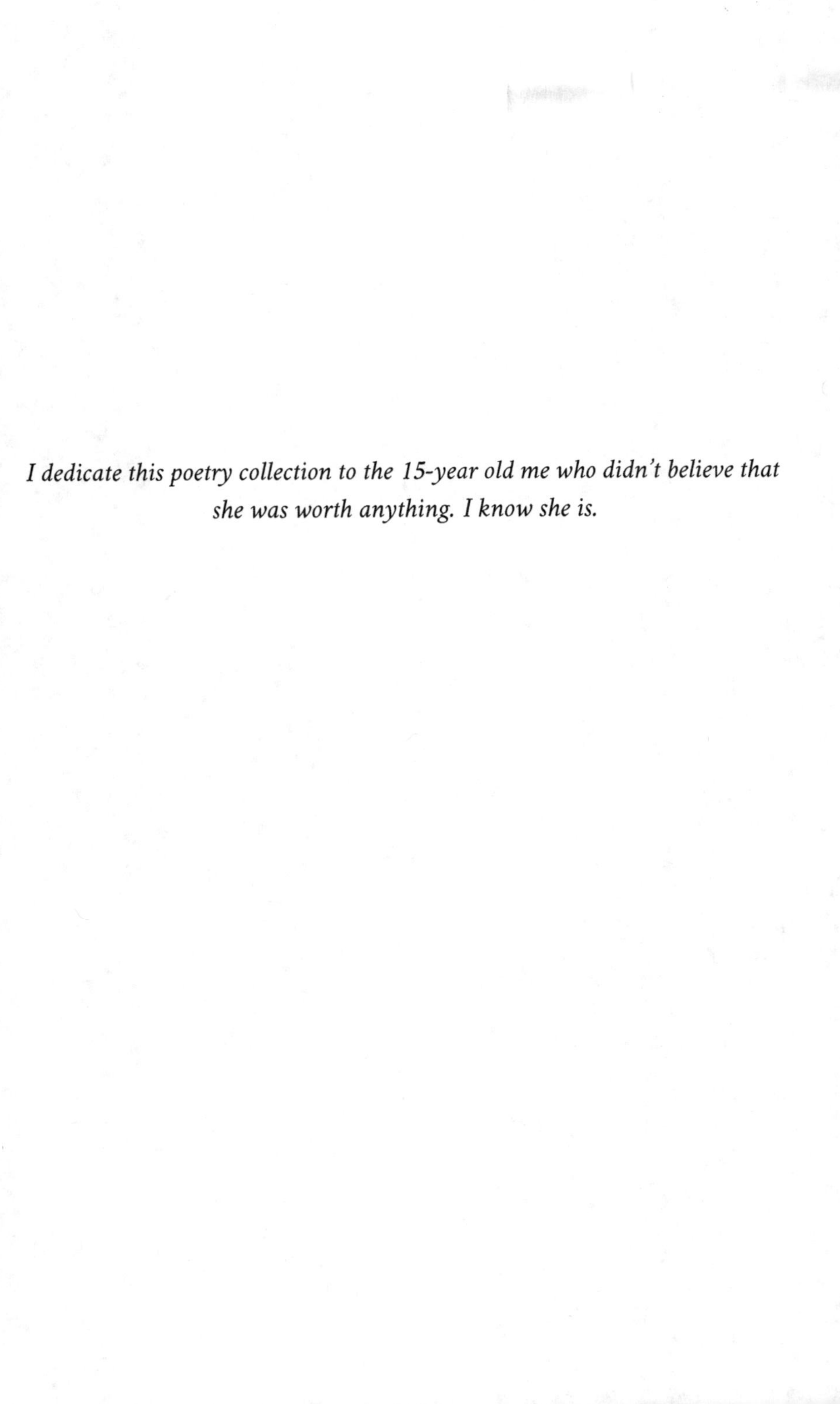

I dedicate this poetry collection to the 15-year old me who didn't believe that she was worth anything. I know she is.

"The more I see, the more I grow, the less and less I seem to know. Only that Life is just a balancing act"

-Achinoam Nini (Noa)

Contents

Preface

This is a short poetry collection that I wrote during my darkest teenage years. Days when I saw no light at the end of the tunnel and when there was a deafening longing for sleep and never wake up. I wrote this to begin healing and to let out my feelings. I hoped that I would live through it so that I could one day publish them and share them with those who struggle the same way I did, and still do. I wrote because whenever I wrote I felt lighter, even if it was just a little. But I haven't had the courage to publish or share my poems until now for fear of getting ridiculed and for fear that no one would find them worth reading.

If you are one of those people who recognise yourself in my poems and find them worth reading, I'd like to thank you. I also want you to know that there is help to get and that writing whatever you're feeling right now is the first step in the process of healing your heart, mind, and soul. Life is hard. We don't let ourselves admit that as often as we should. We tend to instead compare our lives with those around us, or those we deem less fortunate than us. It is okay to be sad, it is okay to not want to get out of bed in the morning. Feelings are what makes us human. We are allowed to hurt, just as much as we are allowed to heal and be happy.

Depression is an illness that we collectively need to discuss more. But these poems aren't about depression, but what life feels like with depression. If you have a loved one going through depression, they might or might not recognise themselves in what I was feeling. Depression and the way it affects our life is unique for every soul. It hurts differently, harms differently, and heals differently. Through my depressed lens, I hope to share an understanding and compassion for all of us. Living is hard. Life is hard. It bears repeating. I learned to be compassionate towards myself little by little, to have more understanding of why I am like this. I hope that you will take these poems, read them in a quiet, comfortable place and let yourself feel whatever you want to feel. Give in and then breathe out.

Remember: Life is just a balancing act

I

Sleepless Nights

Monologue

When darkness falls and the birds become quiet at last, that's when evil comes out. From the tiniest holes, it spreads across our land, leaving nothing but despair and regret in the heart of men. It transforms into what we love and adore the most, ruining us from the inside to the outside. Everyone tries to flee in terror but no one can escape its thorns. Rip, destroy and torture you it will do, till you obey its every wink, making you nothing more than a servant to its powers. You will beg for mercy until you die. You will always feel bad about your choices in life, the choices that became your fall.

Searching for the centre of it all is meaningless. It cannot be found nor fought. It's alive and indestructible, never to die.

The dreams you found, the dreams that left... They are lost for all eternity thanks to your stupidity, my friend. Dreams that could've been your reality are now invisible to your eyes. Those glowing red eyes of yours; that can only see the misery in the world, even in your own home. The home where you once felt love, safety, and peace has turned into the hell you tried to escape. You're trapped in it as the slave you are, without a way out. There's no way out for you. You, my friend, look in the mirror and tell me what you see. It is the image of the person you once were or is it simply what you've had the pleasure to turn out to be? You believe in the good and evil of men but you have never thought that the lord would choose *you*. There isn't a single chance that you would've gotten away. All the goodness and the innocence you had in you as a child are since long gone.

Lie down on your bed, think for a while, and then die. Just die. Simply close your eyes and feel your heartbeat slow down till there's no more left. No way back, no road in front. You shall die on the platform where you were first born. Alone. No friends, family, or animals. Not even a snail will turn its head to look at your sad excuse of an existence, my dear.

You are nothing. You are nothing. You are nothing… anymore…

II

Die to Live or Live to Die

Reasons

There's no reason for my tears
    There's no guilt in my body
    There's no thought in my mind
    There's no will in my heart

I can't just sit here
    I can't just cry here
    I have to get up!
    I have to do what I have to do

The bright light hurts my eyes
    The couch's fabric rubs my arms
    Makes them red and useless
    The air is thick and without oxygen

I feel light-headed
    I feel so stuck
    I have no will
    I have no life

I just lay here on the couch

Waiting for the time to start moving again
But that's not correct at all!
Time is moving! I'm just not moving with it!

For me, the time is still
The day can't become night
The hours cannot pass
Unless I feel it do so first

I'm thinking about my speech
About the future, it has to be
What future? I think to myself
Tomorrow, in an hour, ten years?!

Stop saying that it will be okay
Stop saying that I'm able to do it
That I'm able to change what awaits me
All I know for the future is that I'll die

I won't get up from this couch
Not do all my homework
And get that exam at the end of the year
I'll just lay here still, in silence, and wait

Wait for the time to start moving
And wait for my life to begin
Wait for the will to come back
And wait for my departure…

I'm just laying here…
Crying and crying

Slowly, but surely
Every second I'm dying

Angel

I feel like an angel with a broken wing
   Nothing I do ever seems to be enough
   I'm tired of looking up for help
   To then only see it cloud before my eyes

I can't fly above those horrible clouds
   Blocking my way to find the path home
   I have to stay down here
   A place where all I see is hate, despair, and sadness

If I didn't have the love for you
   Then I'd be lost without a way out
   But the problem I'm struggling with
   Is so hard to overcome and test my every cell

I originally don't want to feel it
   Because it makes me feel so alone
   While I'm wandering down here
   You just have to be up there, so unreachable

If maybe I could find new wings
   I might be able to fly up to you

But finding new wings means the worst
I would have to do everything and anything

Risk my whole life just for you
    Can't you come and save me instead?
    Why do you have to put me through this pain?
    Isn't there any way for you to come find me?

Are my wings forever broken?
    Feel the suffering, my heartache
    Be a lost soul in this hell
    A simple little angel without her wings

III

What you don't know

What life is

One plus one equals two.
  I am born…

The sky is blue in our eyes.
  I learned to crawl…

The sun is the centre of our solar system.
  I learn to talk…

There are seven continents on earth.
  I go to school…

Islam, Judaism, and Christianity are religions.
  I am on my own…

If you drop a stone, it will fall due to gravity.
  I need to be remembered…

An elephant is pregnant between 20-22 months
  Will you marry me?

The Eiffel Tower was built in 1887-1889.

Mum! Please come play with us!

Apple was founded by Steve Jobs.
    Miss, you are fired…

Bogotá is the capital of Colombia.
    What do you want to talk about today?

The Spanish flu killed 1-3% of the world's population.
    I'm sorry, your husband has passed…

Nelson Mandela was South Africa's first president.
    No letters today either madam…

Stefan Holm is a Swedish athlete.
    When I was a little girl…

Carpe Diem means "seize the day" in Latin.
    I always loved living…

Finally, I will close my eyes
    And with a smile on my face
    I shall depart from this world
    With the knowledge I never needed

The only knowledge I would have needed, originally
    Is the simple knowledge we cannot be taught
    The knowledge of living…

Clown Mask

I'm hidden
   I'm gone
   I'm right here
   Can't you see me?

I exist
   I live
   I'm right here
   Can't you see me?

I love
   I hate
   I'm right here
   Can't you see me?

I can feel
   I can hear
   I'm right here
   Can't you see me?

My mask hides it all
   The tears, smiles

And everything in between
  There's no way out

Can someone remove this mask?
  Can't someone see who I am?
  Why do I always have to smile?
  When it's so fake and I cry

Now I understand
  The meaning of
  "Crying without tears"
  You see nothing
  But I feel everything

I can never let go
  Of the mask
  That hides my face

It protects, it hides
  Hides my tears
  Protects my smiles
  And protects me from harm

The clown mask is mine
  My friend to keep and hold

Rose

All roses are beautiful
  The different colours
  They intrigue
  And make you curious

Just like me, a rose is pretty
  But I cannot promise anything
  You could get hurt by me
  For that, I'm not responsible

I will watch as you cry
  I won't understand what I did
  When you tell me you love me
  I will tilt my head confusedly

Don't come too close my love
  I will bite and cut your skin
  Your heart isn't safe close to me
  Your mind is poisoned by my words

I know I am beautiful
  That you want me so badly

But take my advice, please
Believe that just like roses
I have sharp thorns…

IV

Breaking Free

Strings

I feel the strings around me
　　They make my body numb
　　They suppress my mind
　　Until I cannot think

The tears just flow
　　But there's no use to show
　　Anyone my true self
　　Because I'm trapped in hell

During the day I smile like a sunny light
　　But at night the fear comes back
　　And I fall in the fire, burning
　　Trapped in cold, iced wire, turning

I swore to someone
　　That this would end
　　And that the ropes on my limbs
　　Would be cut off for good

As I fall to the ground
　　My tears will come again

But now at least I know
Freedom's grace and warm embrace

When

Crying always helps
    Comforting feels fake
    Talking is a pain
    Hurting is a waste

This time is mine
    This day is ours
    Tomorrow is no one's
    And yesterday is done

If there was a meaning
    If there was a God
    Then why do I hurt
    Like I've been stabbed by something sharp

It should stop
    But it doesn't
    The pain never leaves
    The suffering never ends

But this is not the day
    Nor time

When I give up
I swear that I will stand again

The question is just... When?

V

Burning longing

This isn't love

Whenever I look at you
   All I see is beauty
   Like the colours of a rainbow
   You mesmerize me

I can kiss the ground you walk on
   I can hear the wind that blows in your hair
   I can feel the warmth of the sun, you've felt
   I can see the stars that shape your name

But if I called this love
   Then you'd see what I have seen
   Feel what I felt
   Hear what I heard

But you don't
   You hear her wind
   You see her name
   You feel the warmth from her

I can sit in a corner crying
   Just crying

But instead, I seek you
I stand by to watch you with her

I see your hands together
The pictures you take
I hear your loving words
I want you more than anyone else

This isn't love
This isn't what I deserve
But I will never forget you
And I cannot move on from you

I will love you until you're mine
Or until the day I die
I will want you till I have you
Or till the day you die

"When you have someone
You will forget him/her
When he/she loves you...
Then you won't love him/her"

This is what I tell myself
To think that it's all in vain
Why can't I just admit
This isn't love, just pain
For me...

Time

Time is passing by
   Flying to the sky
   Where it stops and ends
   No one else would know
   The only one who knows is time itself

I am laughing loud
   For a reason, I don't know why
   All I know is that my heart
   Is beating fast

When you call my name in the morning
   Or think of me at night
   I always know it
   My heart is very loved

There might not be many things I see
   Or hear or even listen to
   But I promise that the sound of your voice
   It will always make me fall

Down and down it goes

Will you catch me, please?
Catch me when I reach you
And I promise you my heart
My soul and my everything to you

VI

From me to me...

I'm not changing

I've set my eyes on you
   the adorable innocent you
   I've taken you into my arms
   not knowing where it'll lead

But right now, in this second
   here in my home, my room
   you stand in front of me
   with a smile on your face

I could not believe it
   and God knows I've tried
   I open my mouth to talk
   and tell you all my secrets

You listen with big ears
   smiling at my every word
   and when I am done
   you walk up to me slowly

I can feel your hands
   the softness they bring

makes me weak for real
their touch sets me free

Because I know that you
    love me the way I truly am
    You see past the flaws
    that make me so imperfect

As we join together again
    our bodies as if they are one
    Our minds and hearts unite
    seeing a similar goal at the end

It's amazing how two people
    can connect like this
    As though we're meant to be
    it doesn't change or fail

Our love, my life, and purpose
    will always be the very same
    Equally pure as the white snow
    and with the truth of a tiny child

We won't betray each other
    or leave coldly without a reason
    we'll just fight through it all
    conquer hardships as we go

In this dark, forsaken place
    our love will shine so bright
    find its way through every creek

never to stand down in defeat

Those are the vows I made
    for the one I love the most
    Cry them loudly in delight
    I'll stay by you day as night

You say to me so God-like
    take me for what I am inside
    and ride out into the storm
    with me as your shield in battle

Because I acknowledge, my love
    no one out there will know
    our love exists inside this room
    it's forbidden, yes, God I know
    But I will never stop nor will I give in
    It's not a sin or a choice for us
    we're meant to be, that's the dream
    It's the way it's always going to be…

My insanity

Dreams come true and it's all because of you
Lights go out and the darkness arrives
and it's all because of you, my dream
You, my love, fill my heart with joy
betrayal and despair
All at once and I never saw
how much pain you'd cause me down to my soul
You're a part of my imagination
You're a part of my delusional mind
There's no reason to be scared
There's no reason for you to run
All I ever wanted was for you to be... a part of my insanity

Trees are growing every year
Higher and higher they go up in the sky
If they grow tall enough will God see them too?
When I climb the branches strong will I see the light of the sun once
more?

Is there a way for all this to end?
Will I ever find the path out of this?
Oh will you demon run and disappear

fall into the abyss just like the former me?

You're a part of my imagination
You're a part of my delusional mind
There's no reason to be scared
There's no reason for you to run
All I ever wanted was for you to… a part of my insanity

If you were the end of my road
I would run for all eternity
you are so far away from me and I know that I will never touch your
skin

You're a part of my fantasy
You're a part of my life
There's no fear in your eyes
There's only the love I never had
All I ever wanted was for you to be…
a part of my insanity

But you will never be a part of me

It takes

It takes a year
For your next birthday to come
It takes a month
For your allowance to drop in
It takes a week
For your next weekend to appear
It takes 24 hours
For your day to start over
It takes 8 hours
For you to come home
It takes 1 hour
For the dinner to cook
It takes 30 minutes
For the evening news to end
It can take forever
For you to finally go to sleep

And if you feel like you don't ever have time…then I'll make sure it only takes 1 second for you to know just how much I love you

VII

Being Human

Human

Good and evil were never friends
    Heaven and hell have always been enemies
    But when did humans start their fights?
    When did we become good and bad?

In different countries, people collide
    In different cities gangs declare war
    But this is not a "different world"
    We all live here, on this earth

Why do we scream?
    Why do we hit?
    We shouldn't have to see
    Our wives, husbands, and children die

Blood should flow in our veins
    Not on the streets
    Limbs should be within your body
    Not spread on the field

"We are the smartest beings on this planet"
    Scientists speak on the tv and in books

Yet they can't see the war break out
And the innocent flee from their homes

Suicides are committed
All in vain
Killing becomes an everyday living
For nothing but power

And who owns this power?
No one I can tell
What even is this power?
No one foolish will ever know

The power has become to own a weapon
The power to be able to kill
The power to be the reaper
And decide who's to live and who's to die

I ask you once and for all
Why can't the power be to love,
Understand and above all respect

Respect the living
And respect the dead
Respect each other

And respect yourself